0
zero

zéro

10
ten

dix

20
twenty

vingt

30
thirty

trente

40
forty

quarante

50
fifty

cinquante

60
sixty

soixante

70
seventy

soixante-dix

80
eigthy

quatre-vingt

90
ninety

quatre-vingt-dix

100
one hundred

cent

1000
one thousand

mille

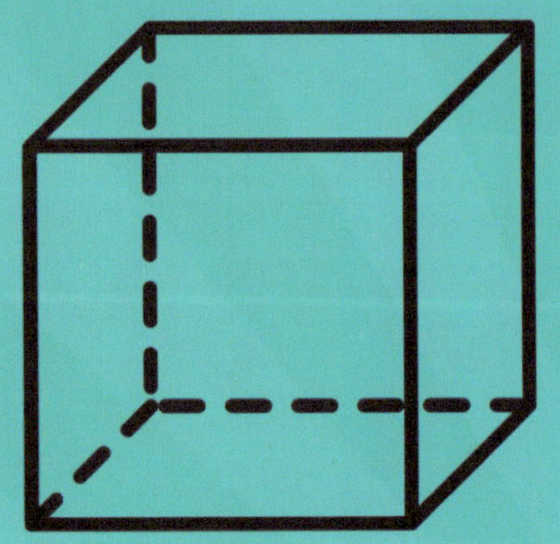

cube

cube

block

bloc

ice cube

glaçon

caramel

caramel

sugar

sucre

dice

dé

gift box

boite cadeau

cardboard box

boîte en carton

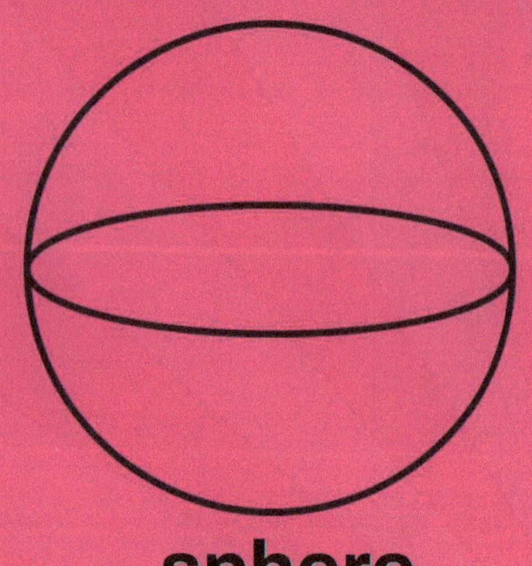

sphere

sphère

ice cream scoop

boule de glace

pearl

perle

bubble

bulle

marbles

billes

planet

planète

snowball

boule de neige

tennis ball

balle de tennis

cylinder

cylindre

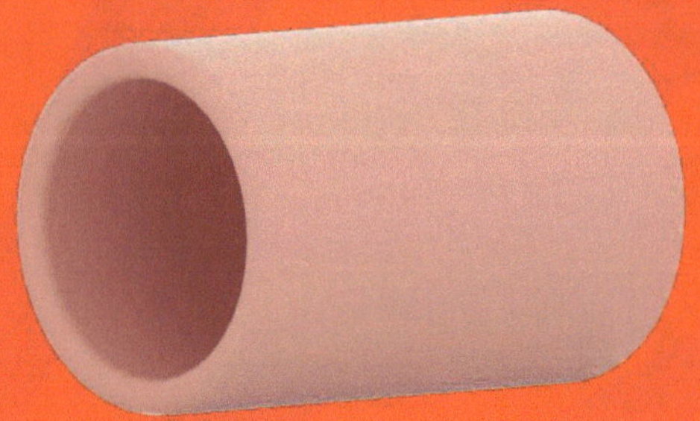

tube

tube

batteries

piles

thread spool

bobine de fil

cinnamon

cannelle

rolling pin

rouleau à pâtisserie

sausage

saucisse

hay bale

botte de foin

cone

cône

road cone

cône de signalisation

ice cream cone

cornet à glace

witch hat

chapeau de sorcière

dungeon

donjon

fir tree

sapin

party hat

chapeau de fête

snail

escargot

blackberry

mûre

currant

🇫🇷 groseille
🇨🇦 gadelle

clementine

clémentine

durian

durian

dragon fruit

🇫🇷 **fruit du dragon**
🇨🇦 **pitaya**

jackfruit

jacquier

star fruit

carambole

asparagus

asperge

radish

radis

red bean

haricot rouge

turnip

navet

cassava

manioc

sweet potato

patate douce

chickpeas

pois chiches

eagle

aigle

bat

chauve-souris

beaver

castor

flamingo

flamant rose

raven

corbeau

blackbird

merle

blue tit

mésange

magpie

pie

swallow bird

hirondelle

lark

alouette

parakeet

perruche

woodpecker

pivert

peacock

paon

parrot

perroquet

toucan

toucan

stork

cigogne

coral

corail

sea anemone

anémone de mer

sea urchin

oursin

seahorse

hippocampe

clownfish

poisson-clown

goldfish

poisson rouge

crab

crabe

hermit crab

bernard-l'ermite

dolphin

dauphin

narwhal

narval

octopus

pieuvre

squid

calamar

whale shark

requin-baleine

orca

orque

blue whale

baleine bleue

beluga whale

béluga

hammerhead shark

requin-marteau

white shark

requin blanc

lemon shark

requin citron

tiger shark

requin tigre

grasshopper

sauterelle

caterpillar

chenille

scorpion

scorpion

lizard

lézard

dinosaurs

dinosaures

black hair

cheveux noirs

ginger hair

cheveux roux

brown hair

cheveux bruns

blond hair

cheveux blonds

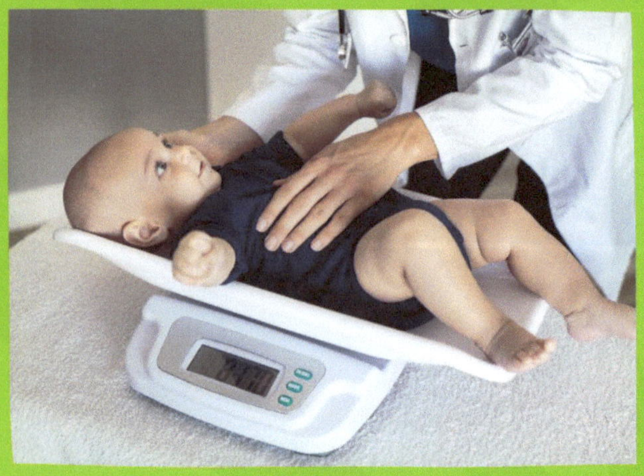

scale

balance

hospital

hôpital

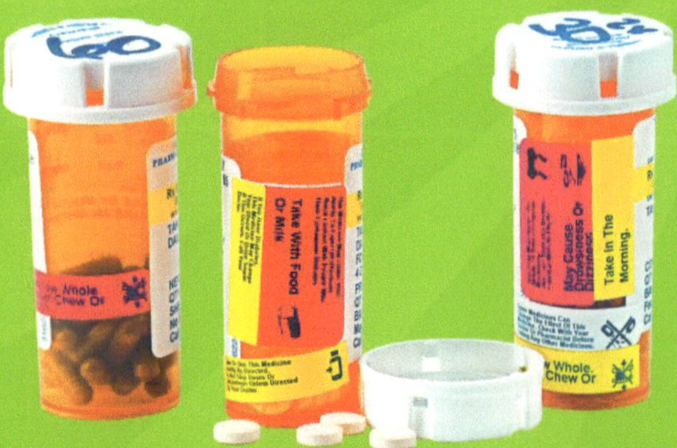

medicine

médicament

thermometer

thermomètre

bandage

pansement

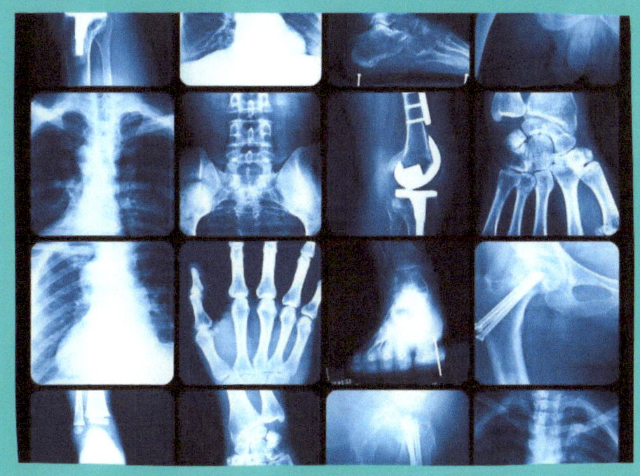

x-ray

radiographie

doctor

docteur

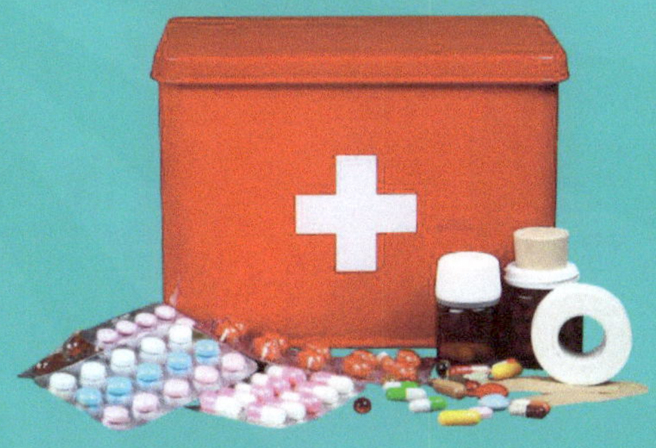

first aid kit

trousse de secours

play

jouer

draw

dessiner

count

compter

write

écrire

dancing

danse

swimming

natation

skiing

ski

basketball

basket-ball

tennis

tennis

ping pong

ping pong

soccer

🇫🇷 football
🇨🇦 soccer

horse riding

équitation

ice hockey

hockey sur glace

judo

judo

boxing

boxe

running

course à pied

baseball

baseball

cricket

cricket

rugby

rugby

volleyball

volley-ball

maracas

maracas

tambourine

tambourin

xylophone

xylophone

violin

violon

piano

piano

guitar

guitare

cello

violoncelle

harp

harpe

drum

tambour

djembe

djembé

drum kit

batterie

trumpet

trompette

horn

cor d'harmonie

saxophone

saxophone

flute

flûte

headphone

casque

sing

chanter

sheet music

partition

microphone

micro

www.ingramcontent.com/pod-product-compliance
Lightning Source LLC
LaVergne TN
LVHW071649180726
843512LV00002B/415